AF480834

CLEAN LIVING, CLEAN SOCIETY

THE VIRTUE OF CLEANLINESS

DR. MINAKSHI BANSAL

Made with ♥ on the Notion Press Platform
www.notionpress.com

DEDICATION

This book is dedicated to all who believe in the transformative power of simplicity and cleanliness. To those who strive daily to leave their environments a little better than they found them—your dedication inspires a brighter, cleaner future for us all.

૭

Contents

Prayer ix

About The Author xi

Preface xv

1. The Basics Of Clean Living: Understanding The Importance Of Cleanliness 1

Part 1

2. Home Sweet Home: Maintaining A Clean And Healthy Household 7

Part 2

3. Personal Hygiene Matters: Essential Routines For Daily Well-being 13

Part 3

4. Green Cleaning: Using Eco-Friendly Cleaning Products 19

Part 4

5. Decluttering Your Space: A Guide To Simplifying Your Environment 25

Part 5

6. Water Wisdom: The Role Of Water In Clean Living 31

Part 6

7. Waste Not, Want Not: Effective Waste Management Techniques 37

Part 7

8. Recycle And Reuse: Turning Old Into New 43

Part 8

9. Eating Clean: Choosing Healthy And Clean Foods 49

Part 9

Contents

10. The Air We Breathe: Improving Indoor Air Quality   55

Part 10

11. Community Cleanliness: Collective Efforts For A Cleaner   61

Society

Part 11

12. Educating The Young: Teaching Children About Cleanliness   67

And Environment

Part 12

13. Health And Cleanliness: Connecting Personal Hygiene To   73

Health Outcomes

Part 13

14. Beauty And Cleanliness: Clean Practices In Personal Care   79

Part 14

15. Workplace Wellness: Keeping Your Work Environment   85

Healthy

Part 15

16. Public Spaces, Public Responsibility: Maintaining Cleanliness 91

In Shared Areas

Part 16

17. The Power Of Plants: Detoxifying Spaces Naturally   97

Part 17

18. Seasonal Cleanliness: Adapting Your Cleaning Habits With   103

The Seasons

Part 18

19. Emotional Cleanliness: Mental Health And Environmental   109

Cleanliness

Contents

Part 19

20. Towards A Cleaner Tomorrow: Building Sustainable Habits   117

Part 20

21. SUMMARY   125

Citation and References   129

Other Books of The Author   131

Contact   133

PRAYER

"Om Bhadram Karnebhih Shrinuyama Devah
Bhadram Pashyemakshabhiryajatrah
Sthirairangais Tushtuvamsastanubhih
Vyashema Devahitam Yadayuh
Svasti Na Indro Vriddhashravah
Svasti Nah Pusha Vishwavedah
Svasti Nastarkshyo Arishtanemih
Svasti No Brihaspatir Dadhatu
Om Shantih Shantih Shantih"

This mantra is a prayer for universal well-being, invoking the blessings of various deities for protection, health, and happiness. It emphasizes the importance of experiencing the auspicious through all senses and living a life aligned with divine purpose. The repetition of "Shantih" at the end signifies a deep desire for peace in the individual, the environment, and the universe at large. This mantra is often recited as a prayer for peace, prosperity, and the physical and spiritual well-being of all beings.

ABOUT THE AUTHOR

Dr. Minakshi Bansal, born in the bustling metropolis of Delhi, India, has led a life steeped in artistry, scholarly pursuit, and an unwavering commitment to societal betterment. Following her marriage, she relocated to Ahmedabad, Gujarat, where she has since blossomed into a multifaceted beacon of inspiration for many. Dr. Minakshi is not only recognized as a gifted artist in the realm of Fine Arts but also as an esteemed author, a devoted social worker and a dedicated research scholar in Psychology. Her journey, marked by a profound dedication to elevating those around her, especially the downtrodden and underprivileged children of society, is a testament to her deep-seated belief in the transformative power of engagement and empathy.

From her earliest days, Minakshi was distinguished by an insatiable appetite for reading. Her literary universe was inhabited by characters and narratives that spanned ethical tales, motivational and inspirational stories, and the mythic parables imbued with life lessons. This voracious reading habit was not merely for personal edification but was driven by a desire to distill and disseminate the essence of these narratives to foster the development of students and peers alike. She was particularly captivated by the lives and teachings of historical figures and spiritual leaders such as Adi Shankaracharya, Swami Vivekananda, Dr. APJ Abdul Kalam, Mahamana Pandit Madan Mohan Malviya, Mahatma Gandhi, Sardar Vallabhai Patel, and Vinoba Bhave, among others. Their philosophies and life stories fueled her ambition to embody their ideals of resilience, selflessness, and relentless pursuit of knowledge.

Dr. Minakshi's academic and practical engagement with psychology has been equally noteworthy. As a research scholar, her focus has been on exploring the intricate tapestry of the human psyche, aiming to unlock the potential for psychological well-being and societal harmony. Her scholarly work is complemented by her active involvement in social work, where she employs her academic insights to make tangible differences in the lives of the underprivileged. Her endeavours in social work are characterized by an innovative approach that combines traditional wisdom with contemporary psychological practices to address the multifaceted challenges faced by these communities.

Her artistic talents, another facet of her diverse capabilities, are not merely a personal passion but also serve as a medium through which she communicates and connects with others. Her art, rich in symbolism and emotional depth, reflects her philosophical inquiries and social concerns, offering viewers a glimpse into the breadth of her intellect and the depth of her compassion.

In addition to her contributions to the arts and social sciences, Dr. Minakshi has embraced the healing arts of Pranic Healing, mastering the techniques developed by Master Choa Kok Sui. This practice, which focuses on the manipulation of Prana or life energy to heal the body and aura, has been both a personal journey of discovery and a means through which she extends her healing touch to others. Her proficiency in Pranic Healing is complemented by her advocacy and teaching of various forms of meditation aimed at rejuvenation, personal betterment, and the cultivation of harmony within individuals and communities alike.

Dr. Minakshi's life is a narrative of relentless pursuit, not just of personal achievement but of the upliftment and empowerment of society at large. Her diverse interests and talents—spanning the arts, literature, psychology, and the healing practices—converge on a singular path of service. She embodies the spirit of the luminaries who inspired her, channelling their legacy through her actions and teachings. Through her books, art, and social initiatives, she continues to inspire a new generation to embark on their own journeys of self-discovery, resilience, and altruism.

Her commitment to social betterment, particularly her focus on uplifting underprivileged children, reflects a deep understanding of the transformative potential of education and personal development. By integrating her knowledge of psychology, her artistic sensibilities, and her healing practices, Dr. Bansal has developed a holistic approach to social work that addresses both the immediate needs and the long-term well-being of the communities she serves.

As an author, Dr. Minakshi's writings offer a blend of inspirational insights, practical wisdom, and reflective contemplations drawn from her extensive reading and life experiences. Her books serve as a guide for those seeking to navigate the complexities of life with grace, resilience, and purpose. Through her narratives, she extends an invitation to her readers to explore the depths of their own potential and to contribute meaningfully to the collective well-being of society.

In Dr. Minakshi Bansal, we find a remarkable synthesis of the artist, the scholar, the healer, and the social activist. Her life's work stands as a beacon of hope and a source of inspiration for individuals seeking to make a difference in the world. Her story is a compelling reminder of the power of individual action, rooted in compassion and driven by a profound commitment to the betterment of humanity. Dr. Minakshi's legacy is not just in the tangible outcomes of her efforts but in the enduring spirit of inquiry, empathy, and service that she embodies.

Preface

In this book, we embark on a journey that intertwines the essence of personal cleanliness with the broader implications for societal welfare and environmental sustainability. It is a discourse shaped not just by the practicalities of maintaining cleanliness but also by a philosophical examination of what it means to live responsibly within our communities.

The motivation for this exploration stems from a simple observation: the state of our surroundings directly influences our health, our behavior, and our attitudes towards each other and the world at large. As we delve into the chapters, we uncover the multifaceted nature of cleanliness, extending beyond mere aesthetics to encompass profound health benefits, both psychological and physical.

Cleanliness is often perceived as a personal virtue, primarily concerned with one's immediate environment. However, as we progress through the discussions, it becomes clear that its significance reaches far beyond individual confines, impacting community health and contributing to the global ecological balance. This book aims to elucidate these connections, providing a comprehensive understanding of why cleanliness is pivotal not only for individual well-being but for the collective good as well.

Each section of the text is dedicated to exploring different dimensions of cleanliness—from the sanctity of personal hygiene and the sanctuaries of our homes to the broader canvases of public spaces and the natural environment. The narrative invites readers to reconsider their daily routines and the products they use, highlighting how sustainable practices can be seamlessly integrated into our lives. By adopting cleaner habits, we not only enhance our health and well-being but also contribute to a more robust and resilient society.

The importance of education emerges as a recurrent theme throughout this book. Educating ourselves and future generations about the benefits of cleanliness and sustainable living is paramount. It is through awareness and informed action that we can effect meaningful change. This book offers practical advice and strategies to foster a culture of cleanliness that can be adopted by individuals, families, schools, and communities.

We also address the challenges and obstacles that impede our progress towards cleaner living. Economic, social, and technological factors all play roles in shaping our cleanliness practices. By understanding these barriers, we can devise more effective strategies to overcome them and make clean living accessible to everyone.

Moreover, this book does not shy away from the complexities and nuances of implementing widespread changes in habits and attitudes. It discusses the roles of government policies, corporate responsibility, and community initiatives in promoting cleanliness. These multifaceted approaches highlight that no single solution exists in isolation; rather, a concerted effort is required to achieve substantial and lasting impacts.

In crafting this narrative, I have drawn from a wealth of scientific research, case studies, and personal anecdotes to provide a rich and engaging discourse. The aim is to inspire action and reflection on how each of us can contribute to a cleaner, healthier society through our everyday choices.

As you turn these pages, I invite you to reflect on your own practices and consider how you might influence those around you. The journey towards cleaner living is not only about improving our present conditions but also about ensuring a sustainable and vibrant future for coming generations.

This book is a call to action. It challenges each of us to take responsibility for our environments, to rethink our habits, and to embrace a lifestyle that prioritizes cleanliness and sustainability. By doing so, we contribute to a larger, collective effort to nurture a society that values and practices cleanliness not just as a virtue but as a fundamental aspect of living well.

I

The Basics of Clean Living: Understanding the Importance of Cleanliness

Cleanliness is often equated with godliness, underscoring its importance not only in religious texts but also in everyday health and wellness practices. It forms the foundation of a healthy life and a sustainable society. The concept extends beyond just keeping our surroundings clean; it includes personal hygiene, environmental consciousness, and the practices that contribute to maintaining a clean community.

Personal Hygiene and Health

At the core of cleanliness is personal hygiene, which protects us from infections and enhances our quality of life. Regular handwashing, for example, is a simple yet effective way to prevent the spread of many diseases. It removes germs and bacteria that we accumulate through touching surfaces, using public amenities, or coming into contact with others. The global emphasis on handwashing during the COVID-19 pandemic highlighted its significance in disease prevention. Beyond handwashing, daily showers, dental care, and clean clothing are essential aspects of personal hygiene. These practices help eliminate body odors, improve self-esteem, and are crucial for social and professional interactions.

Home Hygiene Practices

A clean home environment is vital for overall wellness. Regularly cleaning and disinfecting surfaces in the home can significantly reduce the presence of harmful bacteria and viruses that can cause illness. This involves not just sweeping and mopping floors but also wiping down high-touch surfaces like doorknobs, light switches, and electronic devices. Ensuring that the kitchen, where food preparation takes place, remains hygienic is particularly critical. This includes washing dishes promptly, disinfecting countertops, and managing perishable groceries properly to prevent foodborne illnesses.

The Role of Cleanliness in Mental Health

Cleanliness also has a profound impact on mental health. A cluttered, dirty, or disorganized space can increase stress and reduce one's ability to focus. On the other hand, clean spaces are visually pleasing and psychologically uplifting. They can enhance mood and mental clarity, reduce stress and anxiety, and even improve productivity. This psychological benefit is why many people feel a sense of accomplishment and relief after cleaning their living spaces.

Environmental Cleanliness

Beyond the confines of personal spaces, environmental cleanliness plays a critical role in community health and well-being. Proper disposal of waste, organized trash collection, and regulated industrial emissions contribute to a healthier environment. Littering, for instance, not only spoils the aesthetic beauty of a community but also poses health risks. Accumulated garbage can attract pests such as rodents and insects that spread diseases. Additionally, chemical pollutants can contaminate soil and water sources, leading to broader ecological damage that affects food sources and biodiversity.

Advocating for Ethical Environmental Practices

The advocacy for ethical environmental practices is crucial in promoting cleanliness. This includes pushing for policies that reduce pollution, enhance waste management systems, and encourage the use of renewable resources. Community participation in cleaning drives, recycling initiatives, and environmental education also plays a vital role in maintaining cleanliness at a societal level. By instilling a sense of responsibility towards the environment, individuals can contribute to larger efforts aimed at sustainability.

Sustainable Practices for Everyday Living

To integrate cleanliness into daily living, adopting sustainable practices is essential. This includes using products that are environmentally friendly, such as biodegradable cleaners and personal care items that do not contain harmful chemicals. Reducing plastic use, increasing reliance on renewable energy sources, and supporting local clean-up initiatives can also make a significant impact.

Understanding the basics of clean living and embracing its principles is not just about maintaining personal and home hygiene but also about contributing to a wider cultural shift towards environmental consciousness and community health. It is a holistic approach that enhances personal well-being and fosters a sustainable and prosperous society. By prioritizing cleanliness, we lay the groundwork for a healthier, more responsible, and ethically conscious way of life, paving the way for future generations to inherit a cleaner, more sustainable world.

II
Home Sweet Home: Maintaining a Clean and Healthy Household

A clean home is a sanctuary that offers not just comfort but also health and safety. Maintaining a clean and healthy household goes beyond superficial tidiness; it involves deep cleaning practices, regular maintenance, and a commitment to creating a space that promotes well-being for all inhabitants.

Deep Cleaning Essentials

The journey to a clean home begins with a thorough deep cleaning. This involves tackling every corner of the house, from the attic to the basement, ensuring that no nook is left neglected. Deep cleaning extends to washing curtains, scrubbing walls, cleaning under furniture, and clearing out vents. Such detailed cleaning helps in removing dust mites, allergens, and other pollutants that can accumulate over time and potentially cause health issues.

Carpet cleaning is another vital aspect of deep cleaning. Carpets can harbor dust, pet dander, and microbes if not cleaned regularly. Using steam cleaning or professional cleaning services ensures that carpets are not only superficially clean but also free from embedded dirt and bacteria. Similarly, upholstered furniture requires periodic shampooing to remove body oils and stains that can attract more dirt and degrade the fabric quality.

Maintaining a Clean Kitchen

The kitchen, often the heart of the home, requires special attention because it is where food is stored and prepared. Keeping this area clean is critical to prevent foodborne illnesses and pests. Regular cleaning of appliances, such as refrigerators and ovens, helps maintain them in good working order and prevents the build-up of old food residues that can become a health hazard.

Countertops and sinks need daily cleaning with appropriate disinfectants, especially after preparing raw meat or other contaminant-prone foods. Organizing the pantry and regularly checking for expired items are also essential practices that help in maintaining a clean kitchen. These habits prevent the accumulation of clutter and waste, which can attract pests and lead to contamination.

Sanitizing Bathrooms for Health

Bathrooms are high-humidity environments that can foster the growth of mold and mildew. Regular cleaning and sanitization of the bathroom prevent the build-up of soap scum, limescale, and other residues that can harbor bacteria and viruses. It's important to focus on all fixtures including showers, bathtubs, toilets, and sinks. Ventilation plays a crucial role in bathrooms to keep the air fresh and prevent the growth of mold; therefore, ensuring that exhaust fans are working properly or opening windows can help maintain a healthier environment.

Managing Household Waste

Effective waste management is a critical aspect of maintaining a clean home. This includes separating recyclables from general trash and disposing of hazardous waste like batteries and electronics properly. Composting organic waste is a sustainable practice that reduces the amount of garbage sent to landfills and provides excellent material for gardening.

Routine Cleaning Schedules

To keep a household clean and healthy, establishing a routine cleaning schedule is beneficial. This routine can be daily, weekly, or monthly, depending on the area of the house and the tasks at hand. Daily tasks might include wiping down surfaces, managing laundry, and keeping the floors free of debris. Weekly tasks could focus on vacuuming, dusting, and cleaning bathrooms, whereas monthly tasks might include window cleaning, checking for cobwebs in hard-to-reach places, and inspecting home appliances for any signs of malfunction.

Encouraging Family Participation

Maintaining a clean home is not just the responsibility of one person. Encouraging all family members to participate in household chores can distribute the workload and help instill a sense of responsibility and pride in the living environment. This can be achieved by assigning age-appropriate cleaning tasks to children and organizing regular family cleaning days.

Maintaining a clean and healthy household is fundamental to the well-being of its inhabitants. Regular cleaning reduces the risk of disease, helps manage stress, and creates a welcoming environment. By investing in proper cleaning tools, embracing sustainable cleaning practices, and involving the whole family in the upkeep of the home, maintaining cleanliness becomes an achievable and rewarding goal. A clean home not only protects physical health but also supports mental well-being, making it a crucial aspect of a balanced and healthy lifestyle.

III

Personal Hygiene Matters: Essential Routines for Daily Well-being

Personal hygiene is a critical aspect of daily life, impacting everything from personal health to social interactions. It encompasses a range of practices designed to care for one's body and health, prevent disease, and enhance an individual's sense of self-esteem and well-being.

Fundamentals of Daily Personal Hygiene

Daily personal hygiene begins with basic grooming habits that are essential for maintaining good health and cleanliness. This includes bathing or showering, which helps remove dirt, sweat, and bacteria that accumulate on the skin throughout the day. Regular washing not only cleans the skin but also reduces the risk of skin infections, odors, and other hygiene-related conditions.

Hand hygiene is another cornerstone of personal cleanliness. Regular and thorough washing of hands, especially before meals and after using the restroom, is crucial for preventing the spread of infectious diseases. The use of soap and water is effective in eliminating germs, and in situations where these aren't available, alcohol-based hand sanitizers can serve as a good alternative.

Dental care is equally important. Brushing teeth at least twice a day and flossing daily helps prevent tooth decay and gum disease, which can lead to serious health problems if left untreated. Regular dental check-ups are important to maintain oral health and prevent complications that can arise from neglected dental hygiene.

Hair Care and Scalp Health

Hair care is a significant part of personal hygiene that often goes overlooked. Regular washing of hair helps prevent the build-up of oils, skin flakes, and products that can lead to scalp issues like dandruff or scalp dermatitis. Using a shampoo that suits one's hair type and scalp condition, coupled with occasional conditioning treatments, can maintain hair health and appearance.

Skin Care: Beyond Cleanliness

Skin care is not just about keeping the skin clean; it's about maintaining its health, elasticity, and vitality. Moisturizing the skin daily, especially after showers, helps to lock in moisture and protect the skin from becoming dry or cracked. Sunscreen application is essential to protect the skin from harmful UV rays, which can cause skin damage and increase the risk of skin cancer.

Nail Care: Keeping Hands and Feet Neat

Nail care involves keeping the nails clean and trimmed. Unclean nails can harbor dirt and bacteria, leading to infections. Regular trimming, cleaning under the nails, and avoiding biting nails are all practices that contribute to good nail health and hygiene.

Body Odor Management

Body odor can be a significant concern for many people, affecting social confidence and interactions. Regular bathing, use of deodorants or antiperspirants, and wearing clean clothes are effective ways to manage body odor. Choosing clothing materials that breathe well and are suitable for the climate and activity level can also help minimize odors.

Menstrual Hygiene for Women

Menstrual hygiene is crucial for women's health and comfort. Using sanitary products that are changed regularly throughout the menstrual cycle helps prevent infections and ensures that women can continue with their daily activities comfortably and without interruption. Proper disposal of these products is also a key aspect of menstrual hygiene.

Sleep Hygiene: A Vital Part of Personal Care

Sleep hygiene, though often overlooked, is an essential part of personal health. Creating a conducive sleeping environment, maintaining a regular sleep schedule, and engaging in calming activities before bedtime can significantly improve the quality of sleep. Good sleep is crucial for physical health and mental well-being, affecting mood, energy levels, and overall life quality.

Regular Health Check-ups

Regular health check-ups are part of personal hygiene as they help monitor health conditions and catch potential health issues early. These check-ups include visits to a general practitioner, dentist, and other specialists as required. Early detection of health issues through regular check-ups can lead to more effective treatment and a better prognosis.

Maintaining personal hygiene is fundamental to daily well-being. It enhances health, boosts confidence, and impacts how individuals interact with others. By adopting a comprehensive approach to personal hygiene, individuals can ensure they are protecting their health, presenting themselves positively, and contributing to a hygienic and healthy community environment.

IV

Green Cleaning: Using Eco-Friendly Cleaning Products

In recent years, the shift towards green cleaning practices has become more pronounced as individuals and organizations recognize the environmental and health impacts of conventional cleaning products. Green cleaning involves using products and methods that are environmentally friendly and sustainable, focusing on reducing pollution, enhancing indoor air quality, and conserving resources.

Understanding Green Cleaning Products

Green cleaning products are designed to minimize their environmental footprint. These products are typically made from renewable resources, contain biodegradable ingredients, and are free from harsh chemicals that can cause health issues or environmental damage. Unlike traditional cleaning agents that may contain phosphates, chlorine, and artificial fragrances, green cleaning solutions often use natural substances like vinegar, baking soda, and essential oils.

One of the main benefits of using green cleaning products is that they are less likely to cause skin irritation, allergic reactions, or respiratory issues. This is particularly important in homes with children, elderly individuals, or pets, where the health risks associated with conventional cleaning products can be more pronounced.

The Benefits of Green Cleaning

Adopting green cleaning practices offers numerous benefits, not only for the environment but also for the health of individuals using the products. For instance, green cleaners do not emit the volatile organic compounds (VOCs) that many traditional cleaners do. VOCs can contribute to a range of health problems, including headaches, nausea, and even chronic respiratory issues.

Furthermore, eco-friendly cleaning products help preserve aquatic life and water quality. Many conventional cleaning products contain ingredients that can be toxic to marine and freshwater organisms when they wash down drains and enter waterways. By switching to green products, households and businesses can reduce their ecological footprint and contribute to cleaner rivers, lakes, and oceans.

Effective Green Cleaning Techniques

Effective green cleaning goes beyond just choosing the right products; it also involves adopting sustainable cleaning practices. This includes using microfiber cloths instead of paper towels, which reduces waste and enhances the efficacy of cleaning by trapping dirt and microbes more effectively. Additionally, proper dilution of cleaning products can prevent excessive use and minimize chemical exposure, even with eco-friendly products.

Implementing a green cleaning routine also involves focusing on preventive measures to reduce the need for frequent and intensive cleaning. Placing doormats at every entrance can reduce the amount of dirt and pollutants entering a home, while regular decluttering can minimize dust accumulation and improve indoor air quality.

DIY Green Cleaning Solutions

For those interested in taking green cleaning one step further, DIY cleaning solutions can be an effective and economical approach. Simple ingredients like vinegar can act as a natural disinfectant, while baking soda is excellent for scrubbing and neutralizing odors. Lemon juice, with its high acidity, is effective at tackling grease and adding a fresh scent to cleaning solutions. Recipes for DIY cleaners are widely available and can be customized according to personal preferences and specific cleaning needs.

Choosing the Right Green Cleaning Products

When selecting green cleaning products, it is important to look for certifications that indicate the product meets established environmental and health standards. Certifications such as Green Seal, EcoLogo, and the U.S. Environmental Protection Agency's Safer Choice label help consumers identify products that have been rigorously tested and proven to be environmentally safe.

Challenges and Considerations in Green Cleaning

While green cleaning is beneficial, it also presents certain challenges. Some green cleaning products may be more expensive than conventional ones, which can be a barrier for some households and businesses. Additionally, there can be a learning curve associated with using these products effectively, especially for those accustomed to the immediate results provided by chemical-based cleaners.

Despite these challenges, the long-term benefits of green cleaning—reduced environmental impact, improved indoor air quality, and safer living and working spaces—make it a worthwhile investment. By making informed choices and adopting sustainable practices, individuals and organizations can contribute significantly to a healthier environment and a sustainable future.

Green cleaning represents a critical step forward in our collective effort to protect the environment and our health. It aligns with broader sustainability goals, such as reducing chemical usage, minimizing waste, and conserving natural resources. As more people adopt eco-friendly cleaning practices, the cumulative effect can lead to significant environmental improvements, marking a positive shift towards a more sustainable and conscientious approach to cleanliness.

V

Decluttering Your Space: A Guide to Simplifying Your Environment

Decluttering is more than just a cleaning task; it's a transformative process that enhances the functionality and aesthetic of your living or working space. This process involves reducing clutter to create a more organized and serene environment. The benefits of decluttering are manifold, including reduced stress, increased productivity, and an overall improvement in the quality of life.

Understanding the Impact of Clutter

Clutter can have a profound impact on both your physical and mental health. Physically, it makes spaces less efficient and more difficult to clean. Dust, allergens, and pests thrive in cluttered environments, which can exacerbate allergies and other health issues. Mentally, clutter can lead to stress and anxiety; it can overwhelm the senses, distract from important tasks, and impede your ability to focus.

Studies have shown that cluttered spaces can negatively affect your ability to process information and make it harder to relax, both physically and mentally. On the other hand, an organized space can promote a sense of well-being and control, enhancing your mood and mental clarity.

Steps to Effective Decluttering

The decluttering process involves several steps, each designed to help you systematically tackle the mess and reduce your possessions to only what is necessary and meaningful.

Set Clear Goals: Before you begin decluttering, it's important to set specific, achievable goals. Whether it's clearing out a single drawer or decluttering an entire house, having clear objectives helps keep the process focused and manageable.

Create a Sorting System: As you declutter, use a simple system to decide which items to keep, discard, donate, or sell. Items that are frequently used or bring joy should be kept, while those that are broken, outdated, or no longer useful can be disposed of or given away.

Tackle One Area at a Time: Decluttering can be overwhelming if you try to do everything at once. Break the task into smaller, manageable pieces by focusing on one area at a time. This could be a single room, a specific type of item, or even a drawer. Completing small areas creates a sense of accomplishment and motivates you to continue.

Use the Four-Box Method: To keep organized, many find the four-box method effective during decluttering. Label four boxes as "Keep," "Donate/Sell," "Store," and "Trash." As you sort through your items, immediately place them into one of these categories. This method prevents items from being moved from one cluttered area to another and speeds up decision-making.

Maintaining a Decluttered Space

After decluttering, the challenge often lies in keeping the area clutter-free. This requires ongoing effort and the implementation of new organizational habits.

Implement Storage Solutions: Use shelving, baskets, and dividers to keep items organized. Properly designated places for your belongings make it easier to keep surfaces clear and items off the floor.

Adopt a One-in, One-out Rule: To prevent new clutter from accumulating, make it a habit to remove an old item for every new one you bring into your space. This is particularly useful for clothing, books, and toys.

Regular Mini-Declutter Sessions: Schedule regular sessions to go through your spaces and clear out any items that have accumulated over time. This prevents clutter from building up and makes the task less daunting.

Be Mindful of What You Acquire: Prevent clutter from starting by being more selective about what you bring into your home. Avoid impulse buys and consider whether you really need an item before purchasing it.

Psychological Benefits of a Decluttered Space

The psychological benefits of maintaining a decluttered space are significant. A clean and orderly environment can lead to a more peaceful mind, reduced stress levels, and an increased ability to focus. The act of decluttering itself can also be therapeutic, as it involves making decisions and taking control of your environment, which in itself can be empowering.

Community and Environmental Considerations

Decluttering also has broader implications, including community benefits and environmental impact. Donating items can help those in need, and selling items can extend their life, reducing waste. Being mindful of how you dispose of unwanted items can significantly impact the environment and contribute to a more sustainable lifestyle.

Decluttering is not just about creating more space—it's about enhancing the quality of your living environment and, by extension, the quality of your life. A decluttered space promotes efficiency, reduces stress, and can transform your home into a sanctuary of peace and productivity. By embracing the principles of decluttering and implementing sustainable practices, you can maintain a clean, organized, and harmonious environment.

VI
Water Wisdom: The Role of Water in Clean Living

Water is a fundamental element of life, essential not just for survival but for maintaining cleanliness and promoting health. Its role in clean living is pervasive, influencing various aspects of daily life from personal hygiene to household cleaning and even extending to the broader environmental impact. Understanding and appreciating the significance of water in clean living can lead to more sustainable practices and a healthier lifestyle.

Essential for Personal Hygiene

Water is the cornerstone of personal hygiene. It is crucial for bathing, washing hands, brushing teeth, and more. These activities help remove dirt, microbes, and toxins from the body, preventing disease and keeping individuals healthy. Moreover, water plays a vital role in regulating body temperature through sweating and respiration, processes that are essential for maintaining bodily functions and preventing overheating.

Water and Household Cleanliness

In the home, water is indispensable for cleaning—be it washing dishes, laundering clothes, or mopping floors. The effectiveness of water in cleaning stems from its ability to dissolve substances, making it easier to remove dirt and stains. When combined with cleaning agents, water's cleaning power is enhanced, enabling it to tackle grease, bacteria, and grime on various surfaces.

Conserving Water in Daily Use

Despite its abundance, water is a finite resource, and its conservation is integral to sustainable living. Households can adopt several strategies to reduce water usage, thereby contributing to environmental conservation and reducing utility bills. Installing water-efficient fixtures such as low-flow showerheads, toilets, and faucets can significantly cut down water consumption. Fixing leaks promptly, using water-efficient washing machines, and adopting water-wise gardening techniques like drip irrigation and xeriscaping can also contribute to substantial water savings.

The Impact of Water Quality on Health

The quality of water is just as important as its quantity. Consuming or using contaminated water can lead to health issues ranging from gastrointestinal illnesses to severe infections. Ensuring water quality typically involves municipal treatments that include filtration and disinfection. However, individuals can also use home water filters to remove potential contaminants such as lead, pesticides, and bacteria to ensure the water's safety for drinking and cooking.

Water in Cooking and Nutrition

Water is not only vital for cleaning and personal hygiene but also plays a crucial role in cooking and nutrition. It is used for washing fruits and vegetables, cooking, and as an essential ingredient in countless recipes. Moreover, water is critical to digestion and helps transport nutrients and oxygen to cells. Staying hydrated aids in digestion, flushes out toxins, and helps maintain healthy skin.

Hydrotherapy and Health

The use of water for therapeutic purposes, known as hydrotherapy, has been recognized for centuries. Warm water baths can improve circulation, relax muscles, and soothe painful joints. Similarly, cold water therapy can reduce inflammation and stimulate the immune system. Swimming, one of the most effective forms of exercise, combines the benefits of workout and hydrotherapy, promoting cardiovascular health without stressing the joints.

Water and Mental Well-being

The presence of water in any environment can also have calming effects on the mind. The sound of a running stream, the sight of a tranquil lake, or the simple act of taking a warm bath can reduce stress and promote relaxation. Incorporating water elements into living spaces, such as through aquariums or small fountains, can enhance mental well-being and create a serene atmosphere.

Educational and Community Initiatives

Education about water conservation and management can play a pivotal role in fostering water wisdom. Schools and community centers can offer programs that teach water-saving techniques and the importance of water conservation. Community-based initiatives can include rainwater harvesting projects and the restoration of local water bodies, promoting a collective approach to sustainable water use.

Global Implications of Water Conservation

On a global scale, efficient water use and management are critical to addressing the challenges of water scarcity and ensuring that future generations have access to clean water. International cooperation on water management, technology exchange, and supporting water conservation in developing countries are vital steps toward global water sustainability.

Water is a precious resource that plays a multifaceted role in promoting clean living and maintaining health. By understanding and implementing water conservation techniques, ensuring water quality, and appreciating the broader benefits of water, individuals and communities can enhance their health, improve their quality of life, and contribute to the sustainable management of this vital resource. By fostering a culture of water wisdom, society can ensure that this essential element continues to sustain and enrich lives for generations to come.

VII

Waste Not, Want Not: Effective Waste Management Techniques

Effective waste management is crucial for sustainable living, environmental protection, and public health. As populations grow and urbanization increases, the challenge of managing waste efficiently and responsibly becomes ever more critical. By adopting effective waste management techniques, individuals, communities, and governments can reduce the impact of waste on the environment and improve quality of life.

Understanding Waste Streams

Waste can be classified into several types, including municipal solid waste (household trash/refuse), hazardous waste, industrial waste, biomedical waste, and electronic waste (e-waste). Each type requires different handling and disposal techniques to minimize its impact on the environment. Proper segregation of waste at the source is the first critical step in effective waste management. This not only makes recycling and disposal more efficient but also reduces the contamination of recyclable materials, making the recycling process more effective.

Reduction and Reuse

The most effective way to manage waste is not to produce it in the first place. Reducing waste output can be achieved through mindful consumption and efficient use of resources. For example, opting for products with minimal packaging, avoiding single-use items, and choosing reusable over disposable items can significantly cut down waste generation.

Reusing materials is another crucial element in waste reduction. Items that are still functional can be donated, sold, or repurposed instead of being thrown away. This extends the life of the products and reduces the demand for new materials, thereby conserving resources and energy.

Recycling and Composting

Recycling turns materials that would otherwise become waste into valuable resources. By recycling items such as paper, glass, metal, and certain plastics, we reduce the extraction of raw materials, save energy, and decrease greenhouse gas emissions. However, effective recycling requires proper sorting and processing of recyclables to prevent contamination.

Composting organic waste is another effective waste management technique that contributes to waste reduction. By composting kitchen scraps and yard waste, organic waste is converted into a nutrient-rich soil amendment, which can improve soil health and reduce the need for chemical fertilizers.

Technological Innovations in Waste Management

Advancements in technology have introduced various innovative methods to manage waste more efficiently. Techniques such as anaerobic digestion, plasma gasification, and pyrolysis can convert waste into energy, producing biofuel, electricity, and heat. These technologies not only help manage waste but also contribute to energy production, thus double-benefiting the environment.

Hazardous Waste Management

Proper disposal of hazardous waste is crucial for protecting human health and the environment. Hazardous waste includes items like batteries, chemicals, electronic devices, and fluorescent bulbs. Special handling, treatment, and disposal processes are necessary to safely manage these materials. Many regions have specific regulations and facilities dedicated to hazardous waste to ensure it does not contaminate the environment or pose health risks.

E-Waste Management

Electronic waste or e-waste is one of the fastest-growing waste streams in the world, driven by rapid technological advancement and high obsolescence rates of electronic devices. Proper e-waste management is essential to recover valuable materials and prevent environmental pollution caused by hazardous substances found in electronics. Recycling and safe disposal of e-waste are vital processes that need to be carried out under strict regulations to ensure environmental safety.

Community Participation and Education

Effective waste management is not just the responsibility of waste management professionals or government agencies. It requires active participation from every segment of society. Community-based programs that educate and engage individuals in waste reduction, recycling, and composting can significantly improve the overall effectiveness of waste management systems.

Legislation and Policies

Strong legislation and policies are essential to enforce and encourage proper waste management practices. These can include bans on certain types of waste, incentives for recycling, and penalties for non-compliance. Policies that require producers to take back packaging or products at the end of their life cycle, known as extended producer responsibility (EPR), can significantly reduce waste.

Global Cooperation on Waste Management

Waste management is a global issue that requires international cooperation. Sharing technologies, best practices, and successful policies can help improve waste management worldwide, especially in developing countries where waste management infrastructure may be lacking.

Effective waste management is a multifaceted challenge that involves reducing waste generation, enhancing recycling and recovery, and ensuring proper disposal of waste, including hazardous and electronic waste. By adopting a holistic approach that includes education, community participation, technological innovation, and strong policy frameworks, we can significantly mitigate the impact of waste on our environment and health. This not only leads to cleaner and more sustainable communities but also contributes to the conservation of resources and energy, aligning with broader environmental goals and promoting a healthier planet for future generations.

VIII

Recycle and Reuse: Turning Old into New

In a world increasingly burdened by waste and depletion of resources, the principles of recycling and reusing materials are more relevant than ever. These practices are essential components of sustainable living, helping to reduce the environmental impact of waste, conserve natural resources, and lower greenhouse gas emissions.

The Basics of Recycling

Recycling involves the process of collecting and processing materials that would otherwise be thrown away as trash and turning them into new products. This can significantly reduce the consumption of fresh raw materials, curb energy usage, decrease air and water pollution, and lower greenhouse gas emissions.

Materials commonly recycled include paper, glass, cardboard, plastics, and certain metals. Each of these materials can be reprocessed into new products, thereby closing the loop and minimizing the waste that ends up in landfills.

Effective Recycling Practices

To maximize the benefits of recycling, it is crucial to engage in effective recycling practices. This begins with understanding what materials can be recycled and how to sort them properly. Contamination of recyclables, often caused by improper sorting or the presence of non-recyclable materials, can render batches of recyclables unusable. Therefore, educating the public about the correct recycling procedures is essential.

Local recycling programs may vary, and it is important for individuals to familiarize themselves with the specific guidelines provided by their municipal or waste management services. This includes knowing the types of plastics that can be recycled, how to handle electronic waste, and the proper disposal methods for hazardous materials like batteries and chemicals.

The Power of Reuse

Reusing materials is an immediate form of recycling that involves finding new uses for old items instead of discarding them. Reuse can be as simple as using both sides of a piece of paper or as innovative as repurposing an old building for a new function. The practice of reusing not only reduces waste and saves money but also decreases the demand for new products, conserving the energy and materials used in production processes.

Households can incorporate reuse by donating old clothes and furniture, repurposing glass jars as storage containers, or using scrap materials for art projects. Businesses can contribute by refurbishing and reselling used items or by designing products with reuse in mind, such as modular furniture or electronics with replaceable components.

Community Involvement in Recycling and Reuse

Community involvement is pivotal to the success of recycling and reuse programs. Local governments can facilitate community recycling initiatives by providing accessible recycling centers, hosting electronic waste collection days, and supporting educational programs that teach sustainable waste management practices.

Communities can also create reuse centers where individuals can drop off items that are no longer needed but still usable. These centers can serve as free exchange hubs where community members can find useful items, reducing the need for new purchases and encouraging a culture of reuse.

Challenges and Solutions in Recycling and Reuse

Despite the benefits, recycling and reuse face several challenges. One major challenge is the economic feasibility of recycling certain materials. The cost of collecting, sorting, and processing recyclables can sometimes exceed the profits from selling the recycled materials. To address this, governments and organizations can provide subsidies or incentives to support recycling industries.

Another challenge is the quality and demand for recycled materials. Recycled materials often suffer from degradation in quality, which can limit their usability in high-grade applications. To overcome this, research and development are needed to improve recycling technologies that can enhance the quality of recycled products.

Innovations in Recycling and Reuse

Technological innovations have the potential to transform the recycling and reuse industry. Advanced sorting technologies, such as AI-driven robots and infrared scanners, can improve the efficiency and accuracy of sorting recyclables, reducing contamination levels. Innovations in material science, such as developing new composites from recycled materials, can expand the applications for recycled products.

Global Efforts and Impact

On a global scale, the promotion of recycling and reuse is crucial for addressing the world's waste crisis. International cooperation can facilitate the exchange of best practices, innovative technologies, and policies that support recycling and reuse initiatives across borders.

Recycling and reusing materials are pivotal strategies for sustainable waste management. By turning old into new, these practices not only conserve resources and reduce environmental impact but also foster a culture of sustainability that can permeate all levels of society. As technological advances and community involvement continue to grow, the potential for recycling and reuse to make significant environmental contributions promises a greener, more sustainable future.

IX

Eating Clean: Choosing Healthy and Clean Foods

Eating clean involves selecting foods that are minimally processed, rich in nutrients, and beneficial to both health and the environment. This approach to diet and nutrition emphasizes the quality of the foods consumed, focusing on whole foods like fruits, vegetables, whole grains, lean proteins, and healthy fats, while avoiding processed snacks, sugary drinks, and unhealthy fats.

Understanding Clean Eating

The philosophy behind clean eating is simple: consume foods that are as close to their natural state as possible. This means choosing whole fruits instead of fruit juices with added sugars, or opting for whole grains rather than refined grains. The aim is to nourish the body with pure, healthful ingredients that support overall health and well-being.

Benefits of Clean Eating

Clean eating offers numerous health benefits. It can lead to improved heart health due to lower intakes of sodium and unhealthy fats found in processed foods. It also supports weight management as whole foods are generally lower in calories but higher in fiber, which helps keep you feeling full longer. Additionally, this diet can contribute to better blood sugar control due to its emphasis on whole grains and fiber-rich foods, helping prevent the spikes and dips in blood sugar levels associated with processed foods.

Planning a Clean Eating Diet

To effectively adopt a clean eating diet, planning is essential. This involves reading food labels carefully to avoid chemicals, additives, and preservatives. Planning also includes preparing meals at home using fresh ingredients, which allows for complete control over what goes into your food.

Shopping for Clean Foods

When shopping for food, focus on fresh produce and ingredients. Shopping around the perimeter of the grocery store typically keeps you in the fresh food sections, such as fruits, vegetables, meats, and dairy, while avoiding the central aisles where processed foods dominate. Farmers' markets are also excellent sources of clean, locally grown produce and meats.

Incorporating Organic and Non-GMO Foods

Choosing organic and non-GMO foods can be an important part of eating clean. Organic foods are grown without synthetic pesticides or fertilizers, and non-GMO foods are free from genetically modified organisms, aligning with the philosophy of consuming natural and uncontaminated products. While these options might be more expensive, they reflect a commitment to consuming foods that are believed to be safer and more sustainable.

Understanding Food Sources

Knowing where your food comes from is another critical aspect of clean eating. This means not only looking for organic or non-GMO labels but also understanding the sourcing practices of companies that produce the food. Sustainable and ethical farming practices contribute to the quality and nutritional value of the foods you consume.

Cooking and Preparing Meals

Cooking at home is a cornerstone of eating clean. It ensures that you know exactly what is going into your meals and allows you to avoid the added sugars, salts, and unhealthy fats often found in restaurant meals and takeout. Cooking also gives you the flexibility to experiment with natural flavors from herbs, spices, and seasonings rather than relying on processed condiments.

Balancing Macronutrients

A clean eating plan also involves balancing macronutrients—proteins, fats, and carbohydrates—to meet your health needs. Choosing complex carbohydrates like whole grains, lean proteins such as chicken, fish, beans, and legumes, and healthy fats from sources like avocados, nuts, and olive oil can help maintain this balance.

Hydration and Clean Eating

Hydration plays a crucial role in clean eating. Drinking sufficient water is essential for overall health and helps the body process the high fiber intake typical of a clean diet. Avoiding sugary drinks and limiting caffeine and alcohol are also part of maintaining hydration and overall health.

Challenges and Considerations

While the benefits of clean eating are clear, there are challenges to consider, such as the potential higher cost and time investment required for preparing fresh meals. Moreover, rigidly adhering to a clean eating regimen can sometimes lead to dietary restrictions that might exclude important nutrients or lead to an unhealthy fixation on 'pure' foods.

Adapting Clean Eating to Fit Your Lifestyle

Clean eating doesn't have to be all-or-nothing. It can be adapted to fit individual lifestyles and needs. Flexibility is key—incorporating principles of clean eating into your diet gradually can make the transition easier and more sustainable over the long term.

Eating clean is about making informed food choices and focusing on natural, minimally processed foods. This approach not only supports physical health but also encourages a deeper connection with food sources and preparation methods, enriching your overall eating experience. As more people embrace clean eating, it fosters a broader movement towards sustainability and health-conscious living, making it a beneficial choice for both individuals and the environment.

X

The Air We Breathe: Improving Indoor Air Quality

Indoor air quality is a critical component of environmental health, influencing the well-being and comfort of all who inhabit indoor spaces. As modern lifestyles lead to increased time spent indoors, ensuring the air within homes and workplaces is clean and free from pollutants is paramount. Improving indoor air quality involves addressing various sources of pollution, employing effective ventilation strategies, and using air-cleaning technologies.

Understanding Indoor Air Pollutants

The quality of indoor air can be compromised by various pollutants including dust, pollen, mold spores, and volatile organic compounds (VOCs). Other significant pollutants include carbon monoxide, radon, and tobacco smoke. These contaminants can originate from many sources within the home such as building materials, furnishings, household cleaning products, personal care products, and activities like cooking and heating.

Effects of Poor Indoor Air Quality

Poor indoor air quality can lead to a variety of health issues ranging from temporary discomfort such as eye irritation and headaches to more serious long-term conditions like respiratory diseases and heart problems. Certain populations, such as children, the elderly, and individuals with pre-existing health conditions, may be particularly vulnerable to the effects of indoor air pollutants.

Strategies for Improving Indoor Air Quality

Improving indoor air quality requires a multi-faceted approach, tailored to the specific sources of pollution within a given environment. Key strategies include:

Enhancing Ventilation: Increasing the flow of outdoor air into indoor spaces helps dilute accumulated pollutants. This can be achieved by opening windows and doors when weather and environmental conditions permit, or by using mechanical ventilation systems, particularly in areas like kitchens and bathrooms where moisture and odors accumulate.

Controlling Sources of Pollution: Identifying and reducing sources of indoor air pollution can dramatically improve air quality. This may involve selecting building materials and furniture that emit lower levels of VOCs, using exhaust fans during cooking, and avoiding smoking indoors.

Regular Cleaning and Maintenance: Frequent cleaning helps control dust and allergens, while routine maintenance of HVAC systems ensures they are not a source of indoor air contamination. Changing filters regularly, cleaning ducts, and ensuring that equipment is functioning efficiently can prevent the circulation of pollutants.

Using Air Purifiers: In areas where ventilation is inadequate or external pollution levels are high, air purifiers can be used to remove contaminants from indoor air. Devices equipped with HEPA filters are effective at trapping particulate matter, while activated carbon filters can help reduce odors and VOCs.

Monitoring Humidity Levels: High humidity can lead to the growth of mold and mildew, which are significant indoor air pollutants. Maintaining indoor humidity levels between 30% and 50% can prevent the growth of these organisms. Dehumidifiers and air conditioners are valuable tools for managing humidity.

Testing for Radon: Radon is a colorless, odorless radioactive gas that can enter homes through cracks in floors and walls. It is associated with lung cancer, and testing for radon is the only way to assess exposure levels and take corrective action if necessary.

Indoor Plants for Air Purification: While the effectiveness of plants in purifying indoor air is a subject of debate, they can contribute to better indoor air quality by increasing humidity and potentially removing some types of pollutants. Plants also enhance the living environment psychologically and aesthetically.

Education and Awareness

Educating residents and building managers about the sources and impacts of indoor air pollution, as well as strategies for improvement, is crucial. Awareness can drive behavior change, from choosing low-emission products to implementing regular maintenance schedules for HVAC systems.

Regulatory and Building Standards

Building codes and standards also play a significant role in managing indoor air quality. Regulations that mandate the use of low-emission materials in new buildings, require adequate ventilation, and set standards for indoor air quality can help ensure that new constructions are less likely to contribute to indoor air pollution problems.

The Future of Indoor Air Quality

Technological advancements such as smart home systems and IoT devices offer new opportunities for monitoring and improving indoor air quality. These technologies can provide real-time data about air quality levels and system performance, enabling automated adjustments that optimize the indoor environment.

Improving indoor air quality is a critical aspect of ensuring healthy indoor environments. By addressing the sources of indoor pollutants, enhancing ventilation, and using air-cleaning technologies, individuals can significantly reduce the risks associated with poor indoor air quality. As public awareness grows and technology advances, the ability to monitor and manage air quality becomes easier, promoting better health and well-being for everyone in indoor spaces.

XI
Community Cleanliness: Collective Efforts for a Cleaner Society

Community cleanliness is fundamental to fostering a healthy, sustainable, and pleasant living environment. It encompasses a wide range of activities, from street cleaning and waste disposal to greening projects and public awareness campaigns. By involving everyone from local residents to government bodies, communities can significantly enhance their surroundings and quality of life.

The Importance of Community Cleanliness

Clean communities not only look better, but they also promote better health and safety. Cleanliness reduces the presence of pests, decreases the likelihood of diseases, and lessens pollution levels. Furthermore, well-maintained areas can foster a sense of pride among residents, which in turn encourages further community involvement and development. Studies have shown that cleaner neighborhoods tend to have lower crime rates and higher social cohesion.

Community Involvement in Cleanliness Initiatives

Active participation by community members is crucial for the success of cleanliness initiatives. This can include participating in regular clean-up drives, organizing recycling programs, and engaging in beautification projects like tree planting or community gardens. Local schools, businesses, and religious organizations can play a significant role by integrating these activities into their regular programs, thus fostering a culture of cleanliness.

Role of Local Governments

Local governments have a pivotal role in community cleanliness. They can support efforts by providing necessary resources such as trash bins, recycling centers, and regular waste collection services. Additionally, local authorities can enact and enforce laws related to littering, illegal dumping, and other anti-environmental behaviors. Educational campaigns that teach the benefits of cleanliness and proper waste management can also be sponsored by local governments to raise awareness and encourage participation.

Public Spaces and Cleanliness

Maintaining cleanliness in public spaces such as parks, streets, and public buildings is essential. Regular maintenance schedules should be established, and facilities for disposing of waste properly should be readily accessible. Innovations like solar-powered trash compactors, which can hold more waste than regular bins and notify municipal services when full, enhance efficiency and effectiveness in managing public space cleanliness.

Partnerships for a Cleaner Community

Collaboration between different sectors of the community can amplify the impact of cleanliness initiatives. Partnerships between local governments, non-profits, businesses, and resident associations can pool resources, share expertise, and coordinate efforts more effectively. For example, businesses can sponsor clean-up events, provide supplies, or fund the installation of infrastructure like public restrooms and water fountains.

Incorporating Technology in Cleanliness Efforts

Technology can play a crucial role in enhancing community cleanliness. Mobile apps can be used to report issues like illegal dumping or full trash bins directly to local authorities. Geographic Information Systems (GIS) can help in planning and monitoring cleanliness drives, ensuring that resources are used efficiently and areas in need do not get neglected.

Sustainable Practices and Community Cleanliness

Promoting sustainable practices within the community is also a vital aspect of maintaining cleanliness. Encouraging the use of reusable bags, promoting water conservation, and supporting local food sources are ways communities can reduce their environmental impact while maintaining cleanliness. Composting programs can turn organic waste into a resource, significantly reducing garbage volume and improving soil quality for community gardens.

Education and Awareness Campaigns

Educational campaigns can effectively change behaviors related to waste management and cleanliness. These programs can target schools, where children can learn early about the importance of keeping their surroundings clean. Campaigns can also be directed at adults, focusing on practices like proper waste segregation, recycling, and the economic and health benefits of a clean community.

Challenges in Community Cleanliness

Despite the best efforts, challenges such as insufficient funding, lack of public interest, and inadequate infrastructure can hinder cleanliness initiatives. To overcome these challenges, communities need to be innovative in finding solutions that can work within their specific contexts. Grant programs, volunteer drives, and public-private partnerships can provide necessary support.

Community cleanliness is a collective responsibility that requires the participation and commitment of all stakeholders. Through coordinated efforts, the use of technology, and ongoing education, communities can maintain and improve their cleanliness standards. This not only enhances the aesthetic appeal and health of the community but also builds a stronger, more connected society. By investing in cleanliness, communities are investing in their future, ensuring a safer, healthier environment for generations to come.

XII

Educating the Young: Teaching Children about Cleanliness and Environment

Educating children about cleanliness and environmental responsibility is essential for fostering sustainable behaviors that can lead to a healthier planet. These lessons help instill values that children carry into adulthood, influencing their lifestyle choices and interactions with their surroundings. Effective education on these topics involves not only formal teaching in schools but also informal learning at home and in the community.

Importance of Cleanliness Education

Teaching children about cleanliness is crucial for their health and well-being. Proper hygiene practices can prevent the spread of infectious diseases and contribute to the child's overall development and comfort. Moreover, understanding the importance of cleanliness helps children appreciate the cleanliness of their surroundings, which translates into respect and care for their environment.

Environmental Education for Children

Environmental education is equally important as it equips children with the knowledge of how natural systems work and how human activities impact these systems. It also fosters an appreciation for nature and teaches children about the ways they can protect and preserve the environment. This education can help cultivate a generation that is more conscious of environmental issues like climate change, pollution, and biodiversity conservation.

Strategies for Teaching Cleanliness and Environmental Responsibility

Start Early: Introducing concepts of cleanliness and environmental care early in a child's life can set the foundation for good habits. Simple activities like washing hands before meals and after playing outside can be taught as soon as a child is able to understand basic instructions.

Use Age-Appropriate Learning Materials: For younger children, stories, songs, and games can be effective in conveying the importance of cleanliness and caring for the environment. For older children, more detailed discussions about the science behind hygiene and environmental protection can be introduced.

Incorporate Practical Activities: Learning by doing is particularly effective. Activities like planting trees, recycling workshops, and clean-up drives can make the learning process engaging and memorable. These activities not only teach children about environmental stewardship but also about teamwork and community service.

Lead by Example: Children learn a lot by observing adults. Parents, teachers, and other role models who practice good hygiene and show respect for the environment naturally encourage children to adopt these behaviors.

Create a Culture of Cleanliness and Respect for Nature: Schools and families can foster a culture that values cleanliness and environmental responsibility. This can be achieved by integrating these values into the daily routine and making them a part of the school's ethos or family's lifestyle.

School-Based Environmental Education Programs

Schools play a pivotal role in environmental education. Curricula that incorporate environmental science, discussions on current environmental issues, and the impact of human activities on nature can significantly enhance a child's understanding and concern for the environment. Field trips to nature reserves, parks, and botanical gardens further complement classroom learning by providing direct experiences with nature.

Community Involvement in Environmental Education

Community initiatives can greatly enhance the effectiveness of environmental education. Local environmental groups can organize events and activities for children that promote learning about sustainability practices such as waste reduction, recycling, and conservation of natural resources. These initiatives can also provide hands-on learning opportunities that are not possible in a traditional classroom setting.

Challenges to Environmental Education

Despite the benefits, there are challenges in implementing effective cleanliness and environmental education. These can include a lack of resources, insufficient training for educators in environmental topics, and a curriculum that is already overloaded with other subjects. Addressing these challenges requires commitment from educational authorities, adequate funding, and a willingness to innovate in educational approaches.

Technology and Environmental Education

Technology can enhance the teaching of cleanliness and environmental responsibility through interactive apps, online platforms, and multimedia resources that make learning dynamic and accessible. Virtual reality, for example, can bring distant environments right into the classroom, offering a vivid demonstration of environmental degradation and the importance of conservation.

Educating the young about cleanliness and the environment is essential for ensuring a healthier future for both individuals and the planet. By incorporating these lessons into school curricula, family practices, and community activities, we can nurture a generation that is knowledgeable, environmentally conscious, and proactive in maintaining cleanliness and sustainability. This education not only benefits the environment but also enriches the lives of the children, making them more responsible citizens and stewards of the planet.

XIII

Health and Cleanliness: Connecting Personal Hygiene to Health Outcomes

Personal hygiene is a fundamental aspect of daily living that has a direct impact on health outcomes. The connection between cleanliness and health extends beyond simple concepts of keeping the body clean; it encompasses the prevention of infections, the maintenance of a healthy environment, and the promotion of practices that support overall well-being.

The Science of Hygiene and Health

Cleanliness practices such as hand washing, dental hygiene, and regular bathing are critical in controlling the spread of infectious diseases. For instance, handwashing with soap can significantly reduce the incidence of diarrheal diseases and respiratory infections. The simple act of washing hands before eating and after using the restroom can prevent the transfer of bacteria, viruses, and other pathogens that might otherwise enter the body and cause illness.

Dental Hygiene's Role in Overall Health

Dental hygiene is another crucial aspect of personal cleanliness that affects overall health. Poor dental care is linked to numerous health issues, including heart disease, diabetes, and respiratory illness. Regular brushing and flossing remove plaque and bacteria that cause dental decay and gum disease, which, if left untreated, can lead to severe health problems beyond just tooth decay.

The Impact of Personal Hygiene on Skin Health

The skin is the body's largest organ and serves as the first line of defense against external pathogens. Proper skin care, which includes regular cleaning and moisturizing, helps maintain this protective barrier and prevents issues such as acne, dermatitis, and infections. Moreover, maintaining skin integrity is essential in preventing the entry of infectious agents.

Hygiene in the Home: A Necessity for Health

The cleanliness of one's living environment is intrinsically linked to personal health. Regular cleaning of the home helps control the spread of infectious agents and reduces exposure to allergens such as dust mites and pet dander, which can trigger respiratory problems like asthma and allergies. Ensuring that food preparation areas are clean is also critical to preventing foodborne illnesses.

The Role of Cleanliness in Public Health

On a larger scale, public health initiatives often focus on hygiene to control and prevent disease outbreaks. Programs that promote clean water and sanitation services are crucial in reducing the prevalence of diseases such as cholera and typhoid. Public health campaigns that educate communities about the importance of hygiene can lead to significant improvements in community health outcomes.

Hygiene Practices in Healthcare Settings

In healthcare settings, cleanliness and hygiene are paramount for preventing hospital-acquired infections. Rigorous protocols for the sterilization of instruments, regular hand washing by healthcare providers, and the use of personal protective equipment (PPE) are all essential practices that protect both patients and healthcare workers from infection.

Psychological Effects of Cleanliness on Health

The benefits of cleanliness are not limited to physical health; they also extend to mental well-being. Living and working in a clean, organized environment can reduce stress and improve psychological health. Clutter and dirt can trigger anxiety and discomfort, while clean spaces tend to promote feelings of calm and control.

Barriers to Maintaining Good Hygiene

Despite the clear benefits, various barriers can prevent individuals and communities from maintaining good hygiene practices. These barriers may include lack of awareness, poverty, limited access to clean water and sanitation facilities, and cultural practices. Overcoming these challenges often requires targeted interventions that provide resources, education, and support to those in need.

Educational Campaigns and Their Impact

Educational campaigns play a vital role in improving hygiene practices. By raising awareness of the health risks associated with poor hygiene and demonstrating proper techniques, these campaigns can change behaviors and reduce disease rates. Schools, community centers, and public health departments are all critical venues for hygiene education.

Advancements in Hygiene Technology

Technological advancements have also played a role in enhancing hygiene. Innovations such as touch-free faucets, antimicrobial coatings, and advanced water purification systems contribute to higher hygiene standards in both domestic and public settings.

The connection between health and cleanliness is evident across various aspects of life. From personal hygiene practices like handwashing and dental care to the maintenance of clean homes and public spaces, cleanliness is crucial for promoting health and preventing disease. Through education, technological advancements, and public health initiatives, it is possible to improve hygiene practices globally, leading to better health outcomes and enhanced quality of life.

XIV

Beauty and Cleanliness: Clean Practices in Personal Care

Beauty and personal care are deeply intertwined with cleanliness. The rituals we associate with maintaining our appearance—such as skincare, haircare, and general grooming—are not only about aesthetics but also fundamentally about cleanliness. These practices contribute significantly to our overall health, well-being, and how we present ourselves in the world.

The Foundation of Beauty: Skin Cleanliness

Skin cleanliness is the cornerstone of both dermatological health and aesthetic appearance. Proper skin care routines that emphasize cleanliness can prevent a multitude of skin problems, including acne, blackheads, and other dermatological issues. Daily washing with suitable cleansers can remove dirt, oil, and pollutants that accumulate on the skin's surface. Moreover, regular exfoliation helps to remove dead skin cells that can clog pores, leading to dull skin and breakouts.

Moisturizing: Essential to Healthy Skin

After cleansing, moisturizing is essential to maintain the skin's barrier function and prevent dryness and irritation. Using clean, non-comedogenic moisturizers ensures that the skin is hydrated without introducing new contaminants that can clog pores. The choice of moisturizer can depend on skin type, with heavier, oil-based moisturizers suited for dry skin, and lighter, water-based products ideal for oily skin.

Sun Protection: A Key Aspect of Skin Health

Sunscreen is an often underemphasized aspect of skin cleanliness and health. Protecting the skin from harmful UV rays is crucial to prevent sunburn, premature aging, and skin cancer. Sunscreen should be applied liberally and regularly, not just on sunny days but also when overcast, as UV radiation can penetrate clouds.

Hair Care and Cleanliness

Hair cleanliness is another critical aspect of personal care that impacts both health and beauty. Regular washing of the hair and scalp helps remove build-up of sebum, dead skin cells, and environmental pollutants that can lead to scalp issues such as dandruff and seborrheic dermatitis. However, it's essential to balance the frequency of hair washing to avoid stripping the hair of its natural oils, which can cause dryness and breakage.

Choosing the Right Hair Care Products

Selecting the right hair care products is fundamental to maintaining clean, healthy hair. Shampoos and conditioners should match the hair type and scalp conditions. For instance, individuals with oily hair may need a clarifying shampoo to thoroughly cleanse the scalp, while those with dry, brittle hair might require products with added moisture and protective ingredients.

Clean Makeup Practices

Makeup application is another area where cleanliness is crucial. Using clean brushes and sponges, and regularly washing these tools, can prevent the spread of bacteria that can cause skin irritations and infections. Likewise, it is important to check the expiration dates on makeup products, as expired cosmetics can harbor harmful bacteria and lead to skin problems.

Nail Care: Cleanliness Equals Health

Nail care is not only about aesthetics but also about maintaining the cleanliness of the nails to prevent infections. Regular cleaning and proper grooming of nails prevent the accumulation of dirt and bacteria under the nail bed, which can lead to fungal and bacterial infections. Moisturizing the cuticles and keeping the nails trimmed and clean are all practices that contribute to both the beauty and the health of the nails.

The Role of Diet in Beauty and Cleanliness

A clean diet plays a significant role in personal care by impacting skin and hair health. Diets rich in fruits, vegetables, lean proteins, and healthy fats provide the vitamins and minerals necessary for maintaining robust skin and hair. Hydration is equally important; drinking sufficient water helps keep the skin moisturized and flushes toxins from the body, contributing to a clear, vibrant complexion.

Clean Beauty Products

The trend towards clean beauty products is driven by the growing awareness of the link between health, beauty, and cleanliness. Clean beauty products are formulated without harmful chemicals and with a focus on natural ingredients that are less likely to cause irritation and harm to the body and the environment.

Cleanliness is integral to beauty and personal care. Maintaining clean practices in skincare, haircare, makeup, and nail care not only enhances appearance but also supports overall health. By choosing appropriate products, adhering to clean application methods, and following a healthy lifestyle, individuals can ensure that their beauty routines contribute positively to both their aesthetic and their physical well-being. As awareness grows, the movement towards cleaner, healthier beauty products and practices is likely to continue, reflecting a holistic approach to beauty that values health and sustainability.

XV
Workplace Wellness: Keeping Your Work Environment Healthy

Workplace wellness is a critical component of a company's success, affecting not only the health and well-being of employees but also their productivity and the organization's overall performance. A healthy work environment fosters a physically and mentally supportive space that encourages efficiency, creativity, and satisfaction among employees.

Creating a Physically Healthy Workspace

The foundation of workplace wellness begins with the physical environment. Ensuring that the workspace is clean, well-maintained, and ergonomically designed can prevent health issues and enhance comfort. This includes providing quality office furniture that supports posture, such as ergonomic chairs and adjustable desks. Regular cleaning and maintenance of these spaces reduce the accumulation of dust, mold, and other potential allergens that can compromise air quality and employee health.

Air Quality in the Office

Good air quality is paramount in maintaining a healthy workplace. Poor air quality can lead to respiratory problems, allergies, and reduced concentration and energy among employees. To combat this, businesses can invest in air purification systems, maintain HVAC systems to ensure efficient operation, and incorporate live plants that naturally purify the air. Ensuring that the workplace is free from toxic materials and that any chemicals used for cleaning or operations are safely managed is also crucial.

Lighting and Its Impact on Wellbeing

Lighting plays a significant role in employee wellness. Natural light boosts mood, enhances productivity, and maintains the natural circadian rhythms of the body, reducing eye strain and headaches. Where natural light is not sufficient, providing adequate, high-quality artificial lighting is essential. Blue light filters and adjustable brightness settings can help mitigate the fatigue associated with prolonged screen time.

Noise Control in the Workplace

Noise control is another important aspect of creating a conducive work environment. Excessive noise can lead to stress and decrease productivity. Soundproofing materials, the strategic layout of workspaces, and the provision of noise-canceling headphones are effective ways to manage noise levels, especially in open-plan offices.

Promoting Mental Health and Stress Management

Mental health is equally crucial in workplace wellness. Employers can support mental health by creating a workplace culture that values open communication, inclusivity, and support. Initiatives like providing access to mental health resources, offering workshops on stress management, and ensuring that employees have a reasonable work-life balance can help maintain mental wellness.

Nutritional Health at Work

Providing options for healthy eating in the workplace is another important facet of employee wellness. This can be facilitated through offering healthy food choices in cafeterias, providing kitchen facilities where employees can prepare their own meals, and ensuring that water dispensers are available throughout the office to promote hydration.

Physical Activity and Movement

Encouraging physical activity is another way to enhance workplace wellness. This can be done by providing gym facilities, organizing group fitness classes, or implementing sit-stand workstation setups that encourage movement. Even small breaks for stretching or walking can make a significant difference in overall health and energy levels.

Workplace Policies Supporting Health

Policies play a critical role in underpinning the efforts to create a healthy work environment. These might include flexible work hours that help employees balance personal and professional commitments, policies that encourage sick employees to stay home without penalty, and health and safety regulations that ensure the workplace is free from physical hazards.

Continuous Education and Training

Continuous education and training about health and wellness are vital. Regular training sessions on ergonomic practices, mental health first aid, and personal health management can empower employees to take control of their own health and recognize when they or their coworkers might need support.

Feedback Mechanisms and Continuous Improvement

Finally, establishing feedback mechanisms where employees can voice their concerns or suggestions regarding workplace health and wellness can provide valuable insights that help in continuous improvement. Regularly assessing the workplace environment and making adjustments based on employee feedback ensures that the wellness initiatives remain relevant and effective.

Maintaining a healthy work environment requires a holistic approach that addresses both the physical and mental health needs of employees. By investing in a supportive and health-conscious work setting, organizations can reap the benefits of increased employee satisfaction, reduced absenteeism, and greater productivity. These efforts not only contribute to the well-being of individuals but also to the success of the organization as a whole.

XVI

Public Spaces, Public Responsibility: Maintaining Cleanliness in Shared Areas

Public spaces are essential components of community life. They provide areas for social interaction, recreation, and relaxation that are crucial for the well-being of society. Maintaining cleanliness in these shared areas is not only a matter of public health but also enhances the quality of life and promotes pride in the community. The responsibility for keeping these spaces clean is shared among government, businesses, community groups, and individuals.

The Importance of Clean Public Spaces

Clean public spaces are important for several reasons. First, they contribute to the aesthetic appeal of a community, making it more inviting and pleasant to live in or visit. This can have economic benefits, such as attracting tourists and boosting local businesses. Second, clean environments promote healthier lifestyles by encouraging outdoor activities and reducing the spread of diseases. Lastly, the cleanliness of public spaces can foster a sense of community and civic pride, encouraging residents to maintain and improve the quality of their local environment.

Strategies for Maintaining Cleanliness

Maintaining cleanliness in public spaces requires a multifaceted approach that includes regular maintenance, public education, and the involvement of all community members.

Regular Maintenance and Cleaning: This is the most basic and crucial strategy. Local governments typically have the responsibility to ensure that public spaces are regularly cleaned. This includes trash collection, sweeping of streets and pathways, maintenance of public restrooms, and the care of green spaces like parks and community gardens. Ensuring that adequate funding and resources are allocated for these tasks is essential for keeping public spaces clean.

Provision of Adequate Disposal Facilities: One of the key factors contributing to litter in public spaces is the lack of adequate disposal facilities. Providing enough trash bins, recycling bins, and other waste disposal options in strategic locations encourages proper waste disposal by the public. These facilities need to be regularly emptied and maintained to avoid overflow and ensure effectiveness.

Public Education and Awareness Campaigns: Educating the public about the importance of keeping their community clean can have a significant impact. Awareness campaigns can teach individuals about the consequences of littering and the benefits of a clean environment. Schools, community centers, and local media can be valuable partners in spreading this message.

Community Involvement and Volunteer Initiatives: Engaging the community in cleanliness efforts can foster a sense of ownership and responsibility for local environments. Organizing regular community clean-up events, adopting a street or park programs, and other volunteer initiatives can be effective ways to maintain cleanliness and build community spirit.

Enforcement of Litter Laws: Where education and encouragement fail, enforcement may be necessary. Local governments can implement and enforce litter laws that impose fines for littering in public spaces. Effective enforcement requires that these laws be widely communicated and uniformly applied.

Design of Public Spaces: The design of public spaces can influence how they are used and how easy they are to maintain. Designing with maintenance in mind can ensure that spaces are easier to clean and less likely to accumulate litter. This might include the use of durable materials, strategic placement of trash bins, and landscaping that discourages littering.

Partnerships and Collaborations: Partnerships between local governments, businesses, non-profits, and community groups can leverage additional resources and expertise in maintaining public spaces. Businesses, for example, can sponsor clean-up events or contribute resources for maintenance. Non-profits can coordinate volunteer efforts and provide education programs.

Sustainable Practices: Incorporating sustainable practices into the maintenance of public spaces not only keeps them clean but also protects the environment. This can include using eco-friendly cleaning products, implementing water-wise landscaping, and promoting recycling and composting.

Feedback Mechanisms: Implementing systems where the public can report problems like overflowing trash bins or areas that need attention can help local authorities respond more effectively. This can be facilitated through mobile apps, websites, or direct contact channels.

Maintaining cleanliness in public spaces is a shared responsibility that requires the cooperation of all sectors of society. Through regular maintenance, effective community engagement, and the implementation of smart policies and practices, public spaces can be kept clean and welcoming. This not only improves the quality of life but also instills a sense of pride and ownership in the community, encouraging ongoing participation and care for the environment. As communities come together to maintain their shared spaces, they not only create cleaner environments but also strengthen their social bonds.

XVII

The Power of Plants: Detoxifying Spaces Naturally

Incorporating plants into indoor and outdoor spaces goes beyond mere aesthetics. Plants have a profound ability to improve air quality, enhance mental well-being, and contribute to the physical health of individuals. This understanding has led to a growing recognition of the natural detoxifying power of plants, which can absorb pollutants and improve the overall environment.

Natural Air Purification

One of the most significant benefits of plants is their ability to purify the air. Plants absorb carbon dioxide and release oxygen through the process of photosynthesis, but they also can remove toxins from the air. Research by NASA has identified several houseplants that can absorb harmful toxins like benzene, formaldehyde, and trichloroethylene from the air. Examples include the spider plant, snake plant, and various species of palms, which can improve indoor air quality naturally.

Reducing Carbon Footprint

On a larger scale, outdoor plants and trees play a crucial role in sequestering carbon dioxide, thus mitigating climate change. Urban forestry and green spaces in cities can help offset carbon emissions from vehicles and industrial activities. By absorbing carbon dioxide and releasing oxygen, plants not only purify the air but also contribute to cooling the urban environment, which is particularly important in combating the urban heat island effect.

Enhancing Psychological Well-being

Plants have a well-documented positive impact on mental health. The presence of greenery in homes and workplaces can reduce stress, enhance mood, and improve productivity. Studies have shown that interacting with plants can lower blood pressure, reduce anxiety, and promote feelings of well-being. This psychological effect is sometimes referred to as "biophilia," which suggests that humans possess an innate tendency to seek connections with nature.

Improving Humidity and Reducing Dust

Plants naturally increase humidity levels through the process of transpiration. This can be particularly beneficial in dry indoor environments where artificial heating systems are used. Higher humidity levels can reduce the incidence of respiratory distress caused by dry air. Furthermore, plants can help reduce dust levels in the air because their leaves can trap and absorb particles.

Creating Healing Environments

The use of plants in hospital settings and healthcare facilities is gaining popularity due to their therapeutic benefits. Known as 'healing gardens', these green spaces provide patients and staff with a place to relax, reflect, and recuperate. The calming effect of natural environments can significantly enhance the healing process and improve the outcomes of various treatments.

Plants in Urban Planning

Incorporating plants into urban planning is an effective strategy for improving city living conditions. Green roofs, vertical gardens, and tree-lined streets are examples of how urban areas can integrate more natural elements. These features not only detoxify the environment by absorbing pollutants but also provide urban dwellers with much-needed green spaces.

Sustainable Practices with Plants

Using plants as a natural solution for improving air quality and well-being encourages sustainable practices. It reduces the reliance on mechanical air purification systems, which consume energy and can be expensive to maintain. Moreover, gardening, whether indoor or outdoor, promotes a sustainable lifestyle that involves growing one's own food, which can reduce the carbon footprint associated with food production and transportation.

Educational Opportunities

Educating the public about the benefits of plants is essential for encouraging broader adoption of this natural detoxifying method. Schools, community centers, and local governments can organize workshops and events to teach people how to care for plants and how to integrate them effectively into their living and working environments.

Challenges and Considerations

While plants offer numerous benefits, there are challenges and considerations in using them for detoxification. The effectiveness of plants in purifying air depends on the number and types of plants, the size of the space, and the specific pollutants. Careful selection and maintenance of plants are required to ensure they remain healthy and effective at improving air quality.

The power of plants to detoxify spaces naturally is an invaluable asset in the pursuit of health and environmental sustainability. By leveraging the natural capabilities of plants, individuals and communities can enhance their surroundings, promote public health, and contribute to the sustainability of the planet. As awareness of these benefits grows, so too does the integration of plants into everyday life, fostering a greener, healthier future for all.

XVIII

Seasonal Cleanliness: Adapting Your Cleaning Habits with the Seasons

Seasonal cleanliness involves adjusting cleaning practices and routines to match the specific needs of each season. As the environment changes throughout the year, so do the requirements for maintaining a clean and healthy living space. Adapting cleaning habits seasonally not only ensures that homes remain comfortable and sanitary but also helps manage the challenges posed by different weather conditions.

Spring: Refresh and Revitalize

Spring cleaning is a well-known tradition that involves deep cleaning a home from top to bottom. This season is an ideal time to open windows, let fresh air in, and clear out the stagnation of winter. Key tasks include:

Dusting and Vacuuming: As you open windows more often, it's crucial to dust surfaces and vacuum thoroughly to remove allergens like pollen that can accumulate indoors.

Wardrobe Transition: With the change in weather, it's practical to organize and clean out wardrobes, packing away winter clothing and preparing spring and summer outfits.

Window Cleaning: Spring is an excellent time for cleaning windows, both inside and out, to remove the grime accumulated during winter and to clear the way for more sunlight.

Summer: Focus on Freshness and Air Quality

During the hot summer months, the focus shifts to maintaining air quality and managing pests:

Pest Control: Warmer temperatures can bring about an increase in pests. Ensure that all gaps and entry points around the home are sealed and use natural repellents to keep pests at bay.

Humidity Control: High humidity can lead to mold and mildew. Use dehumidifiers where necessary and ensure good ventilation, particularly in kitchens and bathrooms.

Fridge Clean Out: Summer often involves storing more perishables. Regularly cleaning the refrigerator and discarding expired or spoiled food items will prevent odors and bacterial growth.

Fall: Prepare for the Cold

Fall cleaning prepares your home for the colder months ahead. It's a time to focus on efficiency and warmth retention:

Gutter Cleaning: Clean gutters and downspouts to prevent water build-up that can cause damage during the winter.

Heating Systems: Have heating systems serviced and chimneys cleaned to ensure they are operating efficiently and safely.

Deep Carpet Cleaning: Clean carpets to remove the dirt and allergens accumulated over the warmer months. This also helps improve indoor air quality as windows are closed more often.

Winter: Maintain and Protect

Winter requires a focus on maintaining cleanliness and warmth while ensuring that the home remains sealed against the cold weather:

Entryway Cleaning: Keep entryways clean and dry to prevent slippage and protect indoor flooring. Using mats to trap snow, salt, and dirt is particularly effective.

Upholstery and Fabric Cleaning: With more time spent indoors, ensure that upholstery, blankets, and other fabrics are clean and dust-free.

Clutter Management: Managing clutter can also make indoor spaces more comfortable and easier to heat efficiently.

Using the Right Products

Using seasonal-appropriate cleaning products can enhance your efforts. For instance:

Spring and Summer: Use lighter, naturally scented products that contribute to the airiness of the home. Products with citrus or floral scents can amplify the feeling of freshness.

Fall and Winter: Consider using products that sanitize and protect, as cold and flu viruses are more prevalent. Warmer, comforting scents like cinnamon or pine can enhance the cozy feel of your home during these months.

Adapting to Weather Conditions

Understanding how weather conditions affect your home is key to effective seasonal cleaning. For example, areas with high humidity might require more frequent mold inspections, while homes in dusty regions might need more regular air filter changes.

Maintaining Routine

While seasonal tasks are important, maintaining a regular cleaning routine ensures that the home remains manageable and clean year-round. Weekly tasks like vacuuming, dusting, and keeping surfaces clean should be consistent regardless of the season.

Involving the Family

Seasonal cleaning can be a family affair, with tasks assigned to different members according to age and ability. This not only helps distribute the workload but also instills a sense of responsibility and teamwork.

Adapting your cleaning habits with the seasons ensures that your home remains a healthy and pleasant space year-round. Each season brings different challenges and focusing your cleaning practices accordingly can help you maintain a comfortable and efficient home. This proactive approach to cleanliness not only enhances the immediate environment but also helps preserve the long-term integrity and enjoyment of your living space.

XIX
Emotional Cleanliness: Mental Health and Environmental Cleanliness

Emotional cleanliness is an often-overlooked aspect of wellness that intertwines the cleanliness of our surroundings with our mental health. Just as physical cleanliness impacts our physical health, the state of our environments can significantly influence our psychological well-being. Understanding and implementing practices that foster both environmental and emotional cleanliness can lead to improved mental health and a more satisfying life.

The Connection Between Environment and Mental Health

Our surroundings can have a profound impact on our mood, stress levels, and overall mental health. Cluttered, chaotic, or dirty environments can exacerbate feelings of anxiety and depression, while clean, orderly spaces can promote a sense of calm and control. The process of cleaning itself can also be therapeutic, providing not only a sense of accomplishment but also an opportunity to exert control over one's environment.

Psychological Benefits of Clean Spaces

Clean and organized spaces can reduce stress and improve focus. Clutter can be distracting and can significantly hinder our ability to process information and focus on tasks. This is particularly pertinent in work and study environments where concentration is crucial. Moreover, the act of organizing a space can lead to a clearer mind, enabling more efficient decision-making and problem-solving.

Detoxifying Spaces for Mental Health

Detoxifying our living or working environments involves more than just physical cleaning. It includes creating spaces that are conducive to mental relaxation and positivity. This might involve:

Reducing Clutter: Regularly decluttering spaces to keep them manageable and visually appealing.

Incorporating Elements of Nature: Adding plants, maximizing natural light, or using nature-inspired colors and textures can enhance emotional well-being.

Personalizing Spaces: Decorating spaces with items that bring joy or comfort, such as photos of loved ones, artwork, or personal mementos, can create a nurturing environment.

Routine Cleaning and Mental Health

Establishing a routine cleaning schedule can contribute to better mental health by reducing the anxiety associated with a disorganized environment. Routine also adds a sense of predictability and control, which can be particularly comforting in times of stress.

Impact of Aesthetics and Design

The aesthetics of an environment, including its design and cleanliness, can significantly affect emotions and behaviors. Colors, for instance, can influence mood — blues and greens are often seen as calming, while reds might increase energy levels. Similarly, the presence of harmonious elements and clean lines can contribute to a feeling of tranquility.

Mindfulness and Cleaning

Cleaning can be a mindful activity, not merely a chore. Approaching cleaning tasks with mindfulness — focusing fully on the process and the moment — can turn these activities into a form of meditation, helping to clear the mind of clutter and stress.

Emotional Decluttering

Just as we declutter our physical spaces, periodically assessing and decluttering our emotional lives is essential. This involves:

Reflecting on Relationships: Identifying and addressing toxic relationships that may be contributing to stress.

Setting Boundaries: Learning to say no or setting limits to protect one's mental health.

Prioritizing Self-Care: Ensuring that personal needs for relaxation, entertainment, and rest are met.

Therapeutic Spaces

Designing therapeutic spaces within homes or workplaces can further enhance emotional cleanliness. This could include a dedicated quiet area for relaxation, meditation, or reading, which can serve as a sanctuary from the stress of daily life.

Community Cleanliness and Mental Health

The cleanliness of community spaces also impacts mental health. Well-maintained parks, streets, and public facilities encourage social interaction and physical activity, which are both crucial for mental health. Community involvement in maintaining and improving these spaces can also provide a sense of purpose and belonging.

Educational Programs on Environmental and Emotional Cleanliness

Promoting awareness about the link between environmental cleanliness and mental health can be facilitated through educational programs in schools, workplaces, and community centers. These programs can teach practical skills for maintaining clean environments and managing emotional health.

The concept of emotional cleanliness emphasizes the importance of a clean and orderly environment for maintaining mental health. By fostering clean living spaces and practicing emotional decluttering, individuals can create supportive environments that nurture mental well-being. This holistic approach to cleanliness not only enhances our surroundings but also contributes significantly to our psychological and emotional health, fostering a balanced and fulfilling life.

છ

DR. MINAKSHI BANSAL

XX

Towards a Cleaner Tomorrow: Building Sustainable Habits

As global awareness of environmental issues continues to grow, the importance of building sustainable habits becomes increasingly apparent. A cleaner tomorrow hinges on our ability to adopt practices that minimize waste, conserve resources, and foster a harmonious relationship with our natural surroundings. This transformation involves individual actions as well as collective efforts, leading to a more sustainable lifestyle that benefits both the environment and future generations.

Understanding Sustainability

Sustainability involves meeting our own needs without compromising the ability of future generations to meet theirs. This concept encompasses various dimensions, including environmental, economic, and social sustainability, which are interconnected and equally important. Embracing sustainable habits means making decisions that are not only beneficial in the short term but also contribute to long-term health and well-being.

Reducing Waste

One of the fundamental steps towards sustainability is waste reduction. This can be achieved through practices such as:

Refusing unnecessary items: Avoiding single-use plastics, unnecessary packaging, and freebies that do not add value to our lives.

Reducing consumption: Buying less and choosing products that are durable and long-lasting over disposable items.

Reusing and repurposing: Finding new uses for old items instead of discarding them, which can significantly extend their lifecycle and reduce waste.

Recycling and Composting

While reducing waste is crucial, proper disposal of unavoidable waste through recycling and composting is equally important. Effective recycling involves separating waste into correct categories to ensure that materials can be processed and made into new products. Composting organic waste not only reduces the volume of garbage but also produces valuable compost that can be used to enrich soil, reducing the need for chemical fertilizers.

Conserving Resources

Resource conservation is another key aspect of sustainable habits. This includes:

Energy conservation: Implementing energy-efficient practices such as turning off lights when not in use, using energy-efficient appliances, and insulating homes to reduce heating and cooling needs.

Water conservation: Fixing leaks, using water-efficient fixtures, and adopting water-saving habits like taking shorter showers and using rainwater for gardening.

Sustainable Transportation

Choosing more sustainable modes of transportation can significantly reduce one's carbon footprint. This can include:

Using public transport: Taking buses, trains, or other public transit options instead of driving.

Cycling and walking: These not only reduce emissions but also offer health benefits.

Carpooling and ride-sharing: Reducing the number of vehicles on the road decreases traffic congestion and pollution.

Supporting Sustainable Businesses

Choosing to support businesses that practice sustainability can drive wider environmental change. This involves purchasing from companies that:

Use sustainable materials: Opting for products made from recycled or sustainably sourced materials.

Practice ethical production: Supporting fair trade and ethically produced goods that consider the welfare of workers and the environment.

Implement eco-friendly practices: Engaging with businesses that minimize environmental impact in their production and corporate practices.

Community Involvement and Advocacy

Building sustainable habits also involves community action and advocacy. Participating in community clean-up events, advocating for local sustainability initiatives, and educating others about environmental issues are ways to contribute to broader change. Communities that work together can achieve significant environmental improvements and set a precedent for others to follow.

Continuous Learning and Adaptation

Sustainability is an evolving field, and staying informed about new technologies, practices, and ideas is crucial. Continuous learning and willingness to adapt can help individuals and communities stay effective in their sustainability efforts. Attending workshops, reading, and engaging with environmental groups can provide valuable knowledge and insights.

Modeling Sustainable Practices for Others

Leading by example is a powerful way to influence others. By incorporating sustainable practices into daily life and sharing these experiences with friends, family, and colleagues, individuals can inspire others to make similar changes. This ripple effect can amplify the impact of sustainable habits across communities and beyond.

Building sustainable habits is essential for achieving a cleaner, more sustainable future. Through conscious decision-making, resource conservation, waste reduction, and community involvement, individuals can contribute to environmental preservation and ensure that future generations inherit a healthier planet. As these practices become more integrated into daily life, the collective impact can lead to significant environmental benefits, propelling us towards a cleaner and more sustainable tomorrow.

XXI
SUMMARY

The book "Clean Living, Clean Society: The Virtue of Cleanliness" delves into the intricate relationship between individual cleanliness and broader societal and environmental impacts, advocating for a holistic approach to clean living that encompasses personal health, societal welfare, and ethical environmental practices. This comprehensive guide not only provides practical advice for maintaining cleanliness but also explores the philosophical underpinnings of why clean living is essential for a sustainable future.

1. The Foundation of Clean Living

The book begins by establishing the fundamental importance of cleanliness in our daily lives. Clean personal habits such as regular hand washing, proper waste disposal, and routine household cleaning are discussed as essential practices that prevent the spread of diseases and enhance one's quality of life. These practices are not just about maintaining personal health but also about contributing to the health of the community.

2. The Home as a Sanctuary

Focusing on the home environment, the book emphasizes the role of cleanliness in creating a safe and nurturing space. From decluttering and organizing to using eco-friendly cleaning products, the author provides strategies to enhance the cleanliness of living spaces, which in turn improves mental well-being and reduces stress. The home is portrayed as the starting point for clean living habits that extend into the broader community.

3. Public Spaces and Community Responsibility

The discussion expands into the cleanliness of public spaces such as parks, streets, and public transportation. The author argues for a shared responsibility in maintaining these areas, advocating for community involvement through volunteer clean-ups and local government initiatives. The book highlights how clean public spaces contribute to societal welfare by fostering pride and social cohesion.

4. Seasonal Cleanliness and Routine

Adapting cleaning habits with the seasons is presented as a practical approach to maintaining optimal cleanliness throughout the year. Each season brings specific challenges and opportunities for deep cleaning, pest control, and preparation for weather-related issues. The book provides a detailed guide for seasonal cleaning tasks that ensure a healthy living environment year-round.

5. Emotional Cleanliness and Mental Health

An entire section is dedicated to the concept of emotional cleanliness, which involves maintaining a mental environment that promotes health and happiness. The book discusses how a clean and organized space can significantly impact one's mental state, reducing anxiety and fostering a sense of control. It also touches on the therapeutic aspects of cleaning and organizing as activities that can provide emotional relief and satisfaction.

6. Workplace Wellness

Cleanliness in the workplace is analyzed in terms of its impact on productivity and employee well-being. The author offers insights into creating a healthy work environment through proper sanitation, air quality management, and ergonomic setups. Employers are encouraged to implement policies that promote cleanliness and health, including regular cleaning protocols and supportive amenities.

7. Environmental Cleanliness and Sustainability

The book strongly advocates for environmental cleanliness by promoting sustainable habits such as recycling, using sustainable materials, and reducing plastic waste. The importance of choosing environmentally friendly products and practices is emphasized as crucial for reducing one's ecological footprint and contributing to global environmental health.

8. Educating for Cleanliness

A significant focus of the book is on the role of education in promoting cleanliness. The author calls for educational programs that teach children and adults the importance of cleanliness, environmental conservation, and sustainability. By incorporating these topics into school curricula and community programs, the book argues that societies can foster a generation that values and practices cleanliness in all aspects of life.

9. The Global Perspective

The book concludes by addressing the global implications of clean living. It discusses how cleanliness practices can be adapted and implemented in different cultural contexts, emphasizing the need for global cooperation and policy-making that supports cleanliness and sustainability. The author makes a compelling argument for a unified global effort towards a cleaner, healthier planet.

In essence, "Clean Living, Clean Society: The Virtue of Cleanliness" serves as both a practical guide and a philosophical exploration of the importance of cleanliness in modern society. It calls on individuals, communities, and policymakers to embrace clean habits that will lead to a healthier, more sustainable world. Through detailed explanations, practical tips, and a persuasive narrative, the book inspires readers to transform their approach to cleanliness and to recognize its critical role in shaping a better future.

Citation And References

This book represents the culmination of extensive research and meticulous analysis, incorporating a diverse range of sources, including numerous books, scholarly studies, and personal experiences. Additionally, I have scoured various websites to gather relevant information and data essential for the compilation of this work. I have taken every precaution to ensure the accuracy of the information presented and have diligently cited all sources to acknowledge their contributions.

Despite these efforts, the possibility of inadvertent errors remains. I deeply value the insights of my readers and appreciate any feedback that can help identify and rectify such inaccuracies. I encourage you to bring any discrepancies to my attention.

Your feedback is not only welcome but crucial, as it will aid in correcting current editions and enhancing the content of future ones. I am committed to maintaining the highest standards of accuracy and reliability in my work and thank you for your support and understanding.

Additionally, I firmly uphold the principle of freedom of speech and expression as guaranteed under Article 19(1)(a) of the Constitution of India, and I respect the diverse viewpoints and expressions of all readers.

Other Books Of The Author

1. Empowering Minds: A Journey into Women's Self-Discovery and Power
2. The Dynamics of Motivation: Catalyzing Thought into Action
3. Meditation and Mental Well Being: The Path to Inner Peace and Clarity
4. The Psychology of Child Education: Nurturing Future Generations
5. Ethical Enlightenment: A Modern Guide to Living with Integrity
6. Voices of Empowerment: Stories of Women Rising Against Odds
7. Social Psychology in Everyday Life: Understanding Human Connections
8. The Essence of Motivational Speaking: Inspiring Change in Others
9. Balancing Acts: Women, Work, and the Will to Lead
10. Guiding with Grace: Raising Children with Compassion and Awareness
11. The Power of Positive Aging: Embracing Life After Fifty
12. Building Resilient Communities: Social Work in Action
13. The Ethical Educator: Principles for Teaching and Learning
14. From Insight to Impact: Social Psychology for a Better World
15. The Ethics of Empathy: A Guide to Ethical Living
16. The Science of Empowering the Self: Navigating Life's Challenges with Psychological Wisdom
17. The Mindful Conscious Leader: Meditation Techniques for Modern Management
18. Pioneering Spirit: Women's Pathways to Leadership and Empowerment
19. Feeling to Healing: The Role of Emotional Intelligence in Child Development
20. Transformative Talks and Words of Inspiration: Insights into Motivational Oratory

21. The Hidden Path to Ethical Sustainability: Crafting a Greener Tomorrow
22. Spiritual Integrity: Navigating Life with Moral Compassion
23. Clean Living, Clean Society: The Ethics of Cleanliness
24. Patriotic Spirits: Building a Nation on Positive Attitudes
25. Innovative Integrity & Vibrant Visions: The Ethical and Entrepreneurial Spirit of Gujarat
26. Youthful Visions, Endless Possibilities: Inspiring Ethics and Motivation in Children
27. Living Your Legacy: How to Motivate Others by Living Your Values
28. Secret of Healing Conversations: Ethical Practices in Counselling and Therapy
29. Creative Kindness: Crafting a Life of Compassion and Creativity
30. The Power of Appreciation: How Gratitude Can Transform Your Relationships
31. Bhagavad-Gita: Messages
32. Science of Art: The New Frontier of Fashion Modernism
33. Vivekananda's Virtues: A Blueprint for Modern Living
34. Empower Her: Navigating the Path to Women's Entrepreneurship
35. The Boundless Classroom: Innovations in Global Education
36. The Language of Leadership: Communicating with Authenticity and Impact
37. The Warrior's Mantra: Deciphering the Hanuman Chalisa
38. Echoes of Empathy: Transformative Stories of Social Service
39. Artful Living: Cultivating Creativity in Your Daily Routine
40. Finding Your Why: Discovering Your Passions and Charting Your Course
41. The Role of Social Media in Shaping Self-Esteem and Interpersonal Relationships among Adolescents

৵

CONTACT

Dr. Minakshi Bansal
Social Activist
Ahmedabad, Gujarat, Bharat
minakshiindiag20@yahoo.com

|| LOKAHA SAMASTHAHA SUKHINO BHAVANTU ||

• 135 •